CHILDREN'S AUTHORS

CHRISTOPHER PAUL CURTIS

Jill C. Wheeler
ABDO Publishing Company

Clifton Park - Halfmoon Public Library
475 Moe Road
Clifton Park, New York 12065

visit us at
www.abdopublishing.com

Published by ABDO Publishing Company, 8000 West 78th Street, Edina, Minnesota 55439.
Copyright © 2012 by Abdo Consulting Group, Inc. International copyrights reserved in all
countries. No part of this book may be reproduced in any form without written permission from the
publisher. The Checkerboard Library™ is a trademark and logo of ABDO Publishing Company.

Printed in the United States of America, North Mankato, Minnesota.
062011
092011

 PRINTED ON RECYCLED PAPER

Cover Photo: copyright 2009 Thomas Gennara
Interior Photos: Alamy p. 12; AP Images p. 14; Corbis pp. 7, 13; courtesy Flint Public Library p. 9;
    Getty Images p. 17; iStockphoto p. 16; © Scholastic Inc. pp. 19, 21; copyright 2009 Thomas
    Gennara p. 5; courtesy Thomas Wirt pp. 10–11

Series Coordinator: Megan M. Gunderson
Editors: Megan M. Gunderson, BreAnn Rumsch
Art Direction: Neil Klinepier

Library of Congress Cataloging-in-Publication Data

Wheeler, Jill C., 1964-
 Christopher Paul Curtis / Jill C. Wheeler.
    p. cm. -- (Children's authors)
 Includes index.
 ISBN 978-1-61783-046-4
 1. Curtis, Christopher Paul--Juvenile literature. 2. Authors, American--20th century--Biography-
-Juvenile literature. 3. African American authors--Biography--Juvenile literature. 4. Children's
stories--Authorship--Juvenile literature. I. Title.
 PS3553.U6944Z95 2011
 813'.54--dc22
 [B]   1823
                                        2011009740

CONTENTS

REAL-LIFE FAIRY TALE

There is a real-life, happily ever after story in children's books. That fairy tale story belongs to award-winning author Christopher Paul Curtis.

In 2000, Curtis became the first writer to win both the **Newbery Medal** and the **Coretta Scott King Award** in the same year. The awards are two of the biggest prizes in children's literature. Yet, this fairy tale is not about the prizes. It is about the person who won them. Curtis had always wanted to be a writer. But first, he spent 13 years working in a car factory.

Curtis enjoyed a happy childhood in a loving home. Many of his stories reflect this through a focus on the importance of family. Yet he never shies away from showing the challenges he and other African Americans have long faced. His stories include the sting of **racism** and **discrimination**. Even so, they are filled with humor and compassion.

The humor in Curtis's books comes from his own personality. He is outgoing and friendly. His books help readers understand what it has meant to be African American. His stories have won the hearts of thousands of readers.

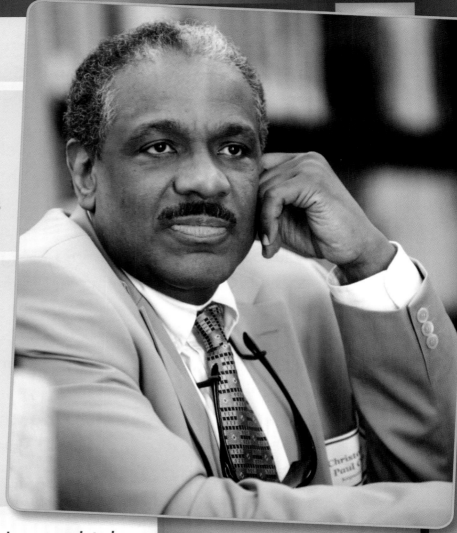

Curtis's writing has been translated into more than 10 languages.

Happy Home, Loving Family

Christopher Paul Curtis was born on May 10, 1953, in Flint, Michigan. Christopher's parents were Herman E. Curtis, Jr., and Leslie Lewis Curtis. Christopher had an older sister named Lindsey. His younger **siblings** were Cydney, David, and Sarah.

Both of Christopher's parents were well educated. His mother had graduated from Michigan State University. She was a homemaker and later a lecturer.

Christopher's father was a **chiropodist**. Yet few people thought to see a doctor who mostly treated feet. And, many were too poor to pay. Plus, America in the 1950s was very **segregated**. At that time, few white people were willing to go to an African-American doctor.

So with few patients and little money, Herman made a tough choice. He applied for a management job with a local factory that made Buick cars. But since he was African American, Herman was only offered a job on the factory floor.

Christopher's hometown is on the Flint River, about 60 miles (95 km) from Detroit, Michigan.

Herman's factory job provided the Curtis family with a comfortable life. Christopher's parents made sure their children grew up surrounded by books. They were loving, but **strict**. The children had to go to bed right after supper. But, they could leave the lights on if they read. It is no surprise that the Curtis children became readers so they could delay bedtime!

Finding a Peaceful Space

Herman and Leslie challenged their children to be the best they could be. They encouraged them to do well in school. And, they shared their belief in the importance of reading.

Christopher's parents were also active in the **civil rights movement**. Sometimes, the Curtis children went with their parents to civil rights activities. Not all restaurants in Flint would hire or even serve African Americans at that time. So, the Curtis family joined in **picketing** those places. And, the family watched news reports of protests in the South.

The Curtis children also joined their father at the public library. Christopher loved the library. He enjoyed spending peaceful Saturdays there, reading anything he could get his hands on.

The only thing Christopher did not like was that there were no stories about kids like him. Nearly all the books were about white children and were written by white authors.

Still, Christopher loved to read.

Christopher read some books, but he especially liked magazines and newspapers. He read *National Geographic*, *Newsweek*, *Sports Illustrated*, and *MAD* magazines. He also liked comic books, especially Batman and Superman. In fact, sometimes his mother would give him ten cents after school for candy. But Christopher would spend it on comic books instead!

FACING RACISM AT SCHOOL

When Christopher was young, he did very well in school. In third grade, he and a classmate became the first African-American students in the Flint public school system to enter a special program for gifted children. Twice a week, they went to a school across town to attend classes.

At home, the Curtis children were often loud and playful. But at school, Christopher was focused and quiet. That did not always keep him out of trouble. When classmates wanted to

Southwestern High School is now known as Southwestern Academy.

pick fights, he would hold them off until Friday. At Christopher's school, that was fight day. Christopher lost just two fights.

In middle school, Christopher's family moved to a new house on the edge of Flint. This was a big change. All of the families in their old neighborhood had been African American. In the new neighborhood, the Curtis family was one of just three.

Christopher's new school had mostly white students and teachers. Not all of them were happy he was there. One teacher gave Christopher an unfair grade simply because of his race. Herman had to speak with the school principal and Christopher's teacher to get the grade changed.

Christopher refused to be defeated by the **racism** he faced at school. In fact, he was elected to the student council in eighth grade! In 1971, Christopher graduated from Southwestern High School.

ON THE FACTORY FLOOR

After graduating, Curtis was accepted at the University of Michigan–Flint. To earn extra money for school, he took a summer job at Fisher Body Plant No. 1. This was where his father worked. Curtis knew he could make a good living at the factory. So, he soon decided to work full time and take just one or two classes at night.

The factory was hot and noisy, and the work was hard. There, Curtis and a partner hung 80-pound (36-kg) doors on Buick cars. However, they eventually figured out how to get twice the breaks.

Because the automobile industry was so important in Flint, the town became known as Vehicle City.

Instead of hanging every other door, each would hang doors for 30 minutes straight. That gave the other a 30-minute break. Then they would switch. Curtis used his breaks to write in a journal. Writing made his 10-hour workdays pass more quickly.

Curtis spent 13 years at the car factory. During that time, he traveled to nearby Ontario, Canada. There, he met a nursing student named Kaysandra Sookram. Curtis wrote her letters after he returned home. Their relationship grew, and eventually they married. They also had two children, a son named Steven and a daughter named Cydney.

LIKE JUMPING OFF A CLIFF

Curtis's writing had always impressed Kaysandra. She supported his decision to become an author.

Curtis had always loved reading and writing. As a child, he had said he would one day write a book. As a young adult, Curtis had thought more and more about writing.

Then in the early 1970s, Curtis read Toni Morrison's novel *Sula*. It inspired him to work harder on his writing. Curtis wrote more and continued taking classes at the University of Michigan. Yet the factory still took most of his time and energy. He knew he needed to quit his job to pursue writing.

Quitting a well-paying job was almost unthinkable for Curtis. Yet in 1985, that's just what he did. He later said it felt like jumping off a cliff.

After the factory, Curtis found a series of low-paying jobs. He worked on a political campaign before realizing he did not like politics. He also worked as a warehouse clerk, a customer service representative, and a maintenance man. Meanwhile, he continued writing and taking classes.

Then in 1990, Curtis won a short story contest. And in 1993, he entered a writing contest at the University of Michigan. He won two Hopwood Awards. After that, Kaysandra suggested that he quit working for a full year and turn one of his winning stories into a book. It was another huge risk, but it was one the Curtis family was willing to take.

A Gamble Pays Off

Originally, Curtis's story was called "The Watsons go to Florida." But then, Curtis was inspired by a poem his son brought home from school. The poem was "Ballad of Birmingham" by Dudley Randall. So, Curtis decided to send his characters to Birmingham, Alabama. His story became *The Watsons Go to Birmingham–1963*.

Curtis's book is about an African-American family that journeys from Michigan to Alabama in 1963. The Watsons face more **racism** in the South than in their home of Flint. While the story is fiction, it includes a real-life event. That is the bombing of Birmingham's 16th Street Baptist Church.

The bombing killed four young African-American girls.

When Curtis took his year off to write, he and his family were living in Windsor, Ontario.

Windsor can be seen just across the Detroit River from Detroit.

This is just across the border from Michigan. At a table in the children's section of the Windsor Public Library, Curtis wrote the book by hand. At the end of each day, Curtis had his son enter his work into the family computer.

Originally, **The Watsons** *wasn't written specifically for children. The publisher suggested that it be changed to appeal to a younger audience.*

In 1993, Curtis entered *The Watsons Go to Birmingham–1963* in a contest **sponsored** by the publisher Random House. The book did not actually qualify for the competition, but the publisher liked it very much. Random House decided to publish it!

The Watsons was published in 1995 and became an immediate hit. Curtis's year of writing had paid off! His book became a **Coretta Scott King Award Honor Book** and a **Newbery Honor Book**. It was also named a *Publishers Weekly* Best Book and a *New York Times Book Review* Best Book.

The following year, Curtis finished his political science degree at the University of Michigan-Flint. He kept writing and published *Bud, Not Buddy* in 1999. Curtis's luck had not run out. The book made history! It won not only a Newbery Medal, but also a Coretta Scott King Award.

Bud, Not Buddy is the story of a 10-year-old boy who sets off during the Great Depression to find his father. The book mixes humor and tragedy as Bud journeys to Grand Rapids, Michigan. There, he hopes to find the jazz musician he's heard is his father.

Curtis used elements from his real life in *Bud, Not Buddy*. A **Negro League** baseball player and a bandleader featured in

Curtis became the first African-American author to win the Newbery Medal since 1976.

the book are based on Curtis's grandfathers. The Hooverville camp for the homeless is based on a field Curtis played in as a child. And, Curtis's daughter wrote the song "Mommy Said No" for the book.

Curtis's success established him as a children's author. And winning the **Newbery** helped his family afford a new home. Most important, this success meant Curtis no longer had to work odd jobs. He could focus completely on writing!

BACK TO THE LIBRARY

As a kid, Curtis loved spy stories. He shared that love of mystery with young readers in his Mr. Chickee detective stories. *Mr. Chickee's Funny Money* and *Mr. Chickee's Messy Mission* were both published in 2005.

The year before, Curtis published *Bucking the Sarge*. This young adult book is set in modern-day Flint. Like Curtis's other award-winning books, it addresses tough topics with humor.

In 2007, Curtis returned to historical fiction. *Elijah of Buxton* is about a young boy in a Canadian settlement of runaway slaves. It won Curtis another **Coretta Scott King Award** in 2008. It also became a **Newbery Honor Book** and won a **Scott O'Dell Award for Historical Fiction**.

Today, Curtis lives in Windsor. He still wakes up at about five o'clock each morning, just as he did when he worked in the factory. He also plays basketball every day, and he likes to watch baseball. Curtis has collected more than 3,000 record albums. And of course, he still loves to read.

Curtis still enjoys writing by hand at a table in a local library. Unlike many other writers, Curtis says he does not usually use outlines to write his stories. Instead, he feels as though his characters tell him what to say. He just writes it down. His fans are looking forward to reading what his characters say next!

Curtis is a frequent speaker at schools and libraries.

GLOSSARY

chiropodist (kuh-RAH-puh-dihst) - someone who provides medical care and treatment for the human foot.

civil rights movement - a movement in the United States in the 1950s and 1960s. It consisted of organized efforts to end laws that involved unequal treatment of African Americans.

Coretta Scott King Award - an annual award given by the American Library Association. It honors African-American authors and illustrators whose work reflects the African-American experience. Runners-up are called honor books.

discrimination - unfair treatment, often based on race, religion, or gender.

Negro League - any of the groups of African-American baseball teams from 1920 to the late 1940s. The teams were formed during a time when African Americans were not allowed to play in the major and minor leagues.

Newbery Medal - an annual award given by the American Library Association. It honors the author of the best American children's book published in the previous year. A Newbery Honor Book is a runner-up to the Newbery Medal.

picket - to participate in a public demonstration or boycott in support of a cause.

racism - the belief that one race is better than another.

Scott O'Dell Award for Historical Fiction - an award that honors the author of an outstanding work of historical fiction for children or young adults.

segregate - to separate an individual or a group from a larger group.

sibling - a brother or a sister.

sponsor - to pay for a program or an activity in return for promoting a product or a brand.

strict - following or demanding others to follow rules or regulations in a rigid, exact manner.

WEB SITES

To learn more about Christopher Paul Curtis, visit ABDO Publishing Company online. Web sites about Christopher Paul Curtis are featured on our Book Links page. These links are routinely monitored and updated to provide the most current information available. **www.abdopublishing.com**

INDEX